# Quilts and Coverlets

from
## The American Museum
## in Britain

*by Shiela Betterton*

**The American Museum in Britain**

ISBN 0 9504971 4 2

Printed in Great Britain by
Butler & Tanner Ltd, Frome and London

# Preface

Several years before the American Museum in Britain was opened in 1961, the co-founders, Dallas Pratt and the late John Judkyn, were collecting American quilted coverlets. In 1957, when they first conceived the idea of establishing an American Museum, Dr Pratt happened to visit the Shelburne Museum in Vermont and saw the quilt collection there, one of the few that had been formed up to that time. Much impressed, he and John Judkyn got permission to include some of the Shelburne quilts in the exhibition of British examples of the craft which Mr Judkyn staged in May 1958 at his Freshford Manor home, four miles from the present Museum. This was possibly the first time American quilts were publicly exhibited in Britain.

The response to this exhibition was so great that it encouraged the two founders to make a feature of quilts in their plan for the new Museum. All this was before a host of private collectors and museums started the great hunt which rooted out thousands of quilts from American attics and interior decorators and textile designers joined in to produce the current apotheosis of patchwork.

From these early beginnings the collection at the American Museum, added steadily to over the years by purchase and gift, has reached a degree of importance which warrants a fully illustrated catalogue bringing to the notice of a wider public the vigorous tradition of American coverlet design and technique and providing illustrated reference for students of the subject to the Museum's collection up to the present time.

**IAN R. M. McCALLUM**

Director
The American Museum in Britain

# Contents

# Introduction

Some of the most striking examples of American needlework are to be seen in the many and varied types of bedcovers which have been made during the past three centuries.

To many people the words patchwork and quilting are synonymous but they are two entirely different forms of needlework. A true quilt is a textile sandwich, with a top layer of fabric, a bottom layer and a filling for warmth, in between. The top may be plain fabric, patchwork, applique or a combination of both techniques. Quilting is the pattern in running stitch which holds the layers together and is the last process in the making of a quilt.

The technique of quilting has been known for hundreds of years, coming from the East, through the Middle East and thence across Europe to Britain and eventually to North America. Early European quilts were purely utilitarian, the stitching being the minimum required to hold the three layers in place. In mediaeval times quilted jackets were worn under metal armour to prevent chafing and light troops had only a quilted jacket for protection. However, it was soon recognised that quilting could be decorative and during the eighteenth century clothing was quilted for warmth – men wore quilted breeches and waistcoats and women quilted petticoats and bodices.

Women from Britain and parts of Europe took with them to America their knowledge of quilting, and up to the time of the American War of Independence American and British 'best' quilts were very similar.

The earliest materials known to have been used for patchwork were the 'painted callicoes' or 'chints' first imported from India in the seventeenth century. At first American cotton manufacturers found it difficult to compete with British and European imports and until the American cotton manufacturing industry got under way in the 1830s, textiles were scarce and expensive and sewing together small scraps in geometric shapes made the best possible use of fabrics. The continuing westward expansion meant that frontier conditions were always present and the need for warm bedding for use in poorly heated homes was a challenge to women to find new ways of piecing together the scraps of material which they so zealously hoarded. However, by the middle of the nineteenth century designing patchwork quilt patterns had become one of the major forms of domestic folk art. The development in America of making one small 'block' or square at a time was economical of time and space and meant the work was easier to handle. However, it needed an artistic eye to visualise the final results when all the small units had been joined together.

It was a tradition that an American girl should have up to twelve quilts in her 'hope chest', possibly thirteen, the thirteenth being her Bride's quilt. She began to piece the 'tops' at a very early age but as a general rule they were not backed and quilted until she became engaged.

Leisure meant time for sewing, and lack of contact with the neighbours meant that women had to rely on pursuits that could be carried out in the home. The majority of quilts would be made and finished at home by the mother and her daughters. Others were quilted at a 'Quilting Bee', which was a welcome social occasion, particularly in the lives of the pioneer women who lived far apart. The women, usually the most experienced needlewomen sat round the quilting frame, and while sewing gossiped and exchanged news. At dusk the frame was put away and the men joined them for supper. The pleasure felt in these gatherings is recorded in many poems and songs.

Patterns for the pieced and applique tops were taken from everyday objects. Women looked at the flowers and foliage around their homes, the tracks of a bird or animal in the earth, even their houses and could see in them the makings of an attractive design. Historical events also gave their names to patterns – Whig Rose reminding us of political events in the early days of the colonies, and Queen Charlotte's Crown called after the last Queen which the colonies had, before becoming the United States of America. Other names were taken from events in the Bible and books such as the *Pilgrim's Progress*, widely read by the early settlers.

The quilting patterns too covered a wide range. Household items such as thimbles, cups, dinner plates and even flat irons were used as a basis for quilting designs. Some had meanings, such as the pineapple as the symbol of hospitality, the pomegranate of fruitfulness and clematis and grapes of prosperity and plenty. It was considered unlucky to sew hearts on anything but a marriage quilt.

This volume shows some of the many and varied bedcovers in the collection of the American Museum in Britain which range in date from the middle of the eighteenth century to the present day. Some of the quilts are named and it may be that the name given is not the usual one for that particular pattern. Visitors to the Museum as well as the Museum Staff have their favourites among the quilt collection and are not slow in bestowing an appropriate name upon them. Thus, the white trapunto quilt which was made by the wife of an officer in the United States Army is always known as 'The Colonel's Lady' coverlet.

# Plain Quilts

It is frequently taken for granted that early American quilts were made of patchwork, but there is no evidence to support this view. It is certain that the art of quilting was taken from Britain and Europe by the first colonists, but no mention is made of patchwork in contemporary literature.

Early textiles were of wool or linen, or a mixture of the two making a fabric called linsey-wolsey. Before the War of Independence, calamanco, a fine worsted fabric which was sometimes glazed, was exported from England and often used for the top of a quilt. Whole fabric was used, often three widths joined together as the first looms were not capable of weaving the whole breadth in one piece. The backing was most often homespun linen or linsey-wolsey with carded sheep's wool for padding. Cotton, which is indigenous to America, did not become a staple crop until the 1760s, so the cotton whole cloth quilts belong to the end of the eighteenth century.

The only patterns on these plain quilts are those formed by the running stitches which hold the three layers in place. Some of these patterns bear a striking resemblance to designs on quilted petticoats, many of which were also made in calamanco.

**Quilt**
L. 99 in   251 cm
W. 78 in   198 cm

The top is made of three pieces of glazed calamanco, indigo dyed. The backing is homespun and the filling of sheep's wool. Quilted with graceful leaf patterns and diagonal lines.

Third quarter of the eighteenth century

A view of a room from Lee, New Hampshire, c. 1730, showing the blue calamanco quilt on the folding bed and a head cloth embroidered in crewel yarns. During the early colonial period the principal bed was in the parlour and showed to advantage the needlewoman's skills.

**Quilt**
L. 94 in    239 cm
W. 90 in    229 cm
*Gift of Miss Agnes and Miss*
*Elizabeth Downs*

Tan glazed linen in strips fifteen and one-half inches wide is used for the top of this quilt, which has a homespun backing and a filling of sheep's wool. The quilting is a graceful overall floral pattern. The two lower corners of the quilt have been cut out so that it would fit easily round the bed posts of a four-poster bed.

Mid eighteenth century

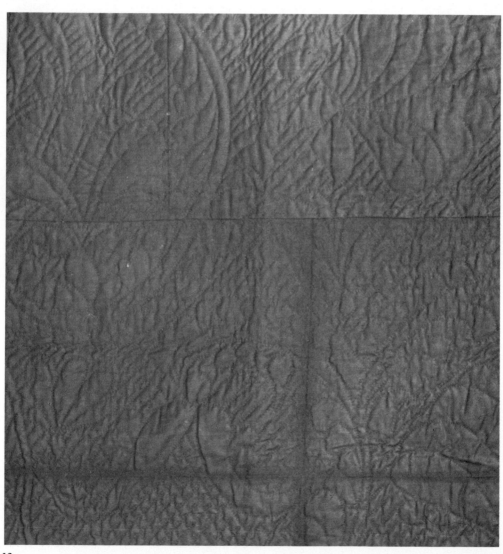

**Quilt**
L. 83 in   211 cm
W. 75 in   191 cm

The cotton and linen twill used for the top of the quilt has been woven in one piece and dyed red after weaving. The pattern with the large central medallion and geometric borders round is very similar to that found on many Welsh quilts.

Late eighteenth century

The Borning Room, 1700/1730, from Lee, New Hampshire.

The true Borning Room dates from earliest times when houses had one room up and one down. A lean-to was added at the back of the house to make a separate kitchen and small extra room to provide privacy and convenience in looking after invalids – the stairs in the earliest houses being little more than ladders. By the middle of the eighteenth century houses were too sophisticated for borning rooms in the true sense but these rooms between kitchen and living room were usually used as extra bedrooms.

**Quilt**
L. 80 in   203 cm
W. 72 in   183 cm

A thick layer of sheep's wool has been used to interline this quilt, which has a red linsey-wolsey top seamed down the centre, and a natural coloured linsey-wolsey backing. The quilting is crudely executed in large stitches using a homespun linen thread.

*c.* 1800

**Quilt**
L. 103 in    262 cm
W.  84 in    314 cm
*Gift of Mr and Mrs H. Dunscombe*
*Colt*

Three breadths of white linen, copper plate printed in blue, have been used to make the top. The backing is also white linen and the simple quilting of diagonal and chevron patterns has been neatly executed.

Although efforts had been made during the seventeenth century to print from copper plates on to cloth, it was not until after 1750 that copper plate printing really got under way. The new technique was first used successfully in Ireland and by 1786 had been mastered by several of the leading London fabric printers. It was a long and expensive process to engrave the design on to the plate, but it made possible the printing of designs with much larger repeats than had been possible with wood blocks and much finer detail could be obtained.

Only one colour was used for the printing – blue, purple or red.

Late eighteenth century

# Pieced Quilts

One of the earliest pieces of known patchwork has been reputedly dated at about A.D. 1000. It was found in a temple in India on one of the old silk routes from China. From that time until about 1700 little is known of patchwork as we know it today, and it was not until fabrics became cheap enough to be cut up before they were quite worn out that patchwork designs began to develop.

The reasons for pieced work were surely repair and economy. The scrap bag was a jumble of old and new fabrics which could be utilised to make the tops of the family bedcovers.

Cutting the pieces and assembling them could be a tedious and exacting process and one in which the whole family joined. Girls were taught to sew at an early age and their first task was usually sewing together squares to make a 'four-patch' or a 'nine-patch' block. The resulting blocks were then put together in some attractive way to make the top. Sometimes there would be a pattern in each block, sometimes a square of solid colour fabric alternated with the pieced block. Straight lines were easy to sew by the inexperienced needlewoman but gradually the skilful blending of colours and shapes enhanced the simple patterns. Boys helped by cutting out the patches and making templates when they were needed. The older girls helped with the quilting.

Early patterns were almost always geometric, making the best possible use of the materials available. The designs could be made by taking a square of material which was folded and cut to make smaller squares. The squares were then cut to make triangles, then all the pieces could be arranged and rearranged to make a design. Once squares and rectangles had been mastered, triangles were attempted, then diamonds. In New England particularly, diamonds were a favourite shape for best quilts.

Patchwork or pieced work became so popular that from about 1830 onwards patterns for quilt blocks were published regularly in an American woman's magazine – *Godey's Lady's Book*. It is interesting to note that in 1835 instructions for making 'honeycomb' patchwork recommended the use of a template and papers and instructed that the patches should be oversewn together, in what is now known as the 'English' method of making patchwork. The 'American' method, where the patches are put right sides together and sewn with a running stitch, was a gradual development.

**TRIANGLES** *could be cut economically from the cloth but were not easy to sew because of the two bias edges. The pattern of the pieced baskets is very similar to one which was used in Tehran nearly five thousand years ago.*

*Small triangles were often used to form an edging called 'Sawtooth' or 'Lend and Borrow'. In other patterns it gives a 'feathered' effect.*

**Red Baskets
Quilt**
L.  67 in    170 cm
W.  81 in    206 cm

The baskets have been pieced from red cotton and white cotton triangles and the handle has been applied. The alternate blocks of white cotton have been expertly quilted with a pineapple pattern.

A quilt with measurements such as these, the width greater than the length, would have been made for a bed with a headboard and footboard and would drop to the floor on either side of the bed.

New Jersey
Nineteenth century

**Orange Baskets Quilt**
L. 80 in 203 cm
W. 64 in 163 cm

The baskets have been pieced and set into blocks placed diagonally, while the flowers and fruit have been applied. The quilting is very fine and close and gives a stippled effect.

Nineteenth century

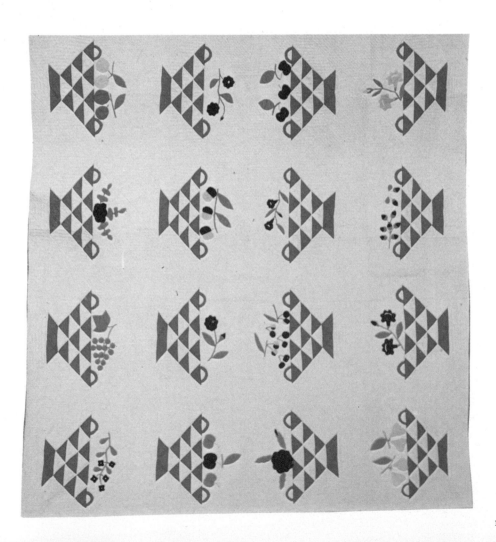

**Cactus Rose Quilt**
L. 81 in    205 cm
W. 78 in    195 cm

Red diamonds and green triangles form the Cactus Rose pattern. The handwoven linen/cotton backing proclaims the quilt's early origin. Neat feather circles have been quilted in alternate blocks.

The placing of the flowers is such that they are upright when viewed from either the top or the bottom of the bed.

Early nineteenth century

**Pine Trees
Quilt**
L. 80 in   203 cm
W. 77 in   196 cm

Red and white triangles used in a slightly different way make the pattern known as 'Pine Trees' or sometimes 'Tree of Life'.

The Pine Tree often appears in American embroidery and patchwork. It symbolises the forests of New England pines which provided masts for the King's ships. One of the first coins struck in the colonies was the Pine Tree Shilling.

Nineteenth century

# Sawtooth Quilt

L. 90 in  228 cm
W. 92 in  231 cm

The top is of white homespun with a sawtooth pattern of late eighteenth-century block printed English cotton. Originally coloured green, yellow, pink and blue, the green and yellow of the print have almost completely faded out. The border is quilted with a running feather pattern.

A label attached to the quilt states that it was made about 1800 by Elizabeth C. Kinzer at New Holland, Lancaster County, Pennsylvania.

**Feathered Star
Quilt**
L. 102 in   259 cm
W.  82 in   208 cm

Although made late in the nineteenth century this quilt is
surprisingly modern in colouring. The feathered star is one of the
classic pieced designs and was a favourite with many quiltmakers
because it gave them an opportunity to show off their skills in
working with tiny triangles. This is not a pattern for the beginner
as the piecing is extremely complex. There is a delicacy about the
pattern which is echoed in the dainty scalloped border and the
neat stitching. Perhaps it was made for a hope chest, as hearts have
been quilted on the points of the large stars.

Nineteenth century

**Swallows
Crib Quilt**
Square: 45 in   114 cm
*Gift of Mrs Paul Moore*

The basis of this pattern is a four-patch block called by some 'Fox and Geese'. The triangles and squares of the basic block can be arranged in several ways making patterns which are variously known as 'Hovering Hawks', 'Flock of Geese', 'The Swallow', and 'The Anvil'. It is interesting to note, however, that the 'Fox and Geese' pattern is sometimes known as 'Old Maid's Puzzle'.

As befits a crib quilt the blocks are quite small – five inches square – and the fabrics are in muted tones, mainly browns and cream with touches of red.

*c.* 1840

**Sailboats**
**Crib Quilt**
L. 40 in 101 cm
W. 35 in 89 cm
*Gift of Mr and Mrs Joel Kopp*

The pieced 'Sailboat' pattern is half of the block used to make 'The Swallow' pattern. The other half of the block is solid colour. This pattern has been made on a diminutive scale suitable for a crib quilt and has been pieced from red-patterned and white cotton. It is neatly quilted.

1845

*The easiest block for the beginner was one which incorporated*
SQUARES *and rectangles as these could be joined with a running
stitch obviating the necessity for templates and papers.*
   *The first pattern which a young girl was taught to sew was a Four-
Patch. When this had been mastered she made a Nine-Patch. The
blocks were assembled to make some attractive pattern for the top.*

**Four-Patch
Quilt Top**
L. 82 in  208 cm
W. 74 in  188 cm
*Gift of Mrs Emerin S. Chute,
grand-daughter of the maker*

Four-patch blocks made from printed calicoes have been banded
with natural coloured calico. This top, which has never been made
into a quilt, was made by Mrs Emerin Price Semple of Louisville,
Kentucky.

Nineteenth century

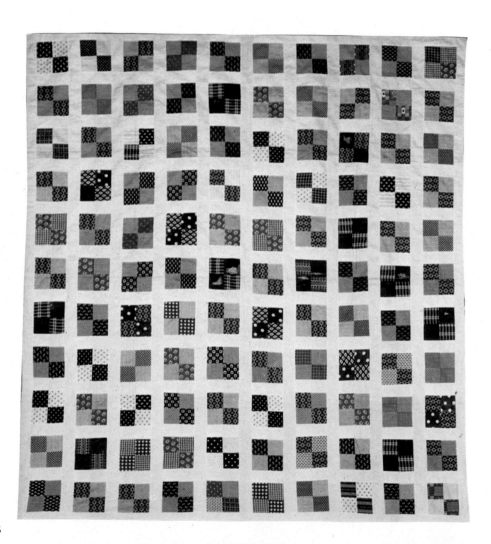

**Strippy
Quilt**
L. 100 in   254 cm
W.  93 in   236 cm
*Gift of Mrs Paul Moore*

Eleven strips have been combined to make the top of the quilt. Five strips composed of nine patch blocks set diagonally with triangles completing the block, alternate with six strips of chintz. The triangles of the centre strip are made of a different chintz to the others. The fabric used is mainly European glazed chintz of the eighteenth century. The edge is bound with a hand-woven tape. Worked in cross stitch on the back are the initials and date 'S.G. 1817'.

**Nine-Patch
Quilt**
L. 84 in   213 cm
W. 80 in   203 cm
*Gift of Mrs Mary Shaw,
grand-daughter of the maker*

A wide variety of early prints have been assembled to make the one-inch squares which form the nine-patch block. A definite colour scheme can be seen in the pattern. The quilting is neat and even. This quilt has a cotton padding in which some of the seeds remain.

Made by Margaretta Boone Wintersteen of Port Carbon, Pennsylvania.

1840/50

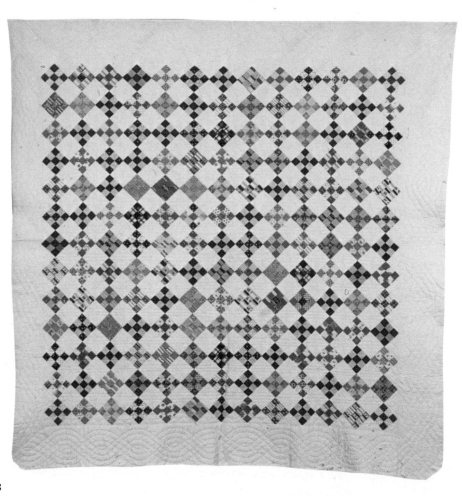

**Nine-Patch**
**Quilt**
L. 90 in   229 cm
W. 85 in   216 cm
*Gift of Mrs Fanny E. Edwards*

Interesting early nineteenth-century cottons have been pieced to make this version of a nine-patch top. Brown and white checked cotton has been used for the backing. This is one quilt where pieces from the family scrap bag could have been used to make the top.

Nineteenth century

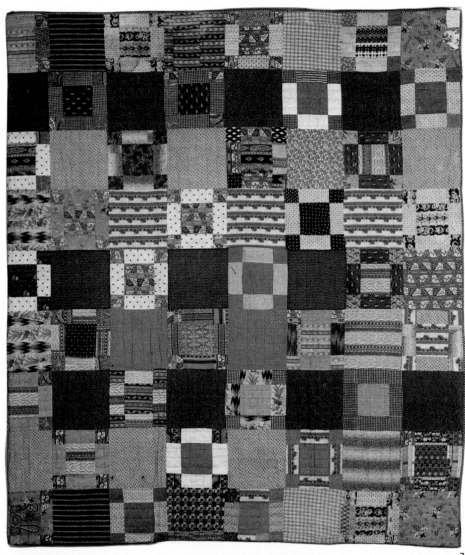

**Quaker Silks
Quilt**
L. 96 in   244 cm
W. 84 in   213 cm

The silks used for the top are typical of those which were used in the making of Quaker dresses. The backing is of bright blue glazed cotton.

The quilt came from the Yarnall family, who were prominent Quakers in Philadelphia. It was customary for such families to employ a sewing woman who came to the house at regular intervals to make new clothes and household articles and to repair old ones. This quilt would have been made by such a sewing woman from the pieces left over from her dressmaking.

*c.* 1834

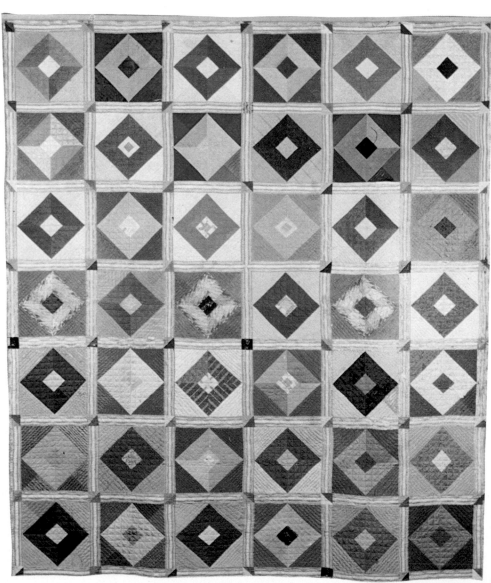

**Double Wedding Ring Quilt**
L. 88 in   224 cm
W. 77 in   196 cm
*Gift of Mrs Virginia McMahan, daughter of the Maker*

As skill is needed in placing all the patches to form perfect circles, this is not a pattern for the beginner. The pattern forms its own scalloped border. Mrs Grace Munschain of Clarkesville, Texas, who made the quilt, saved the pieces from her daughters' dresses over the years.

1930

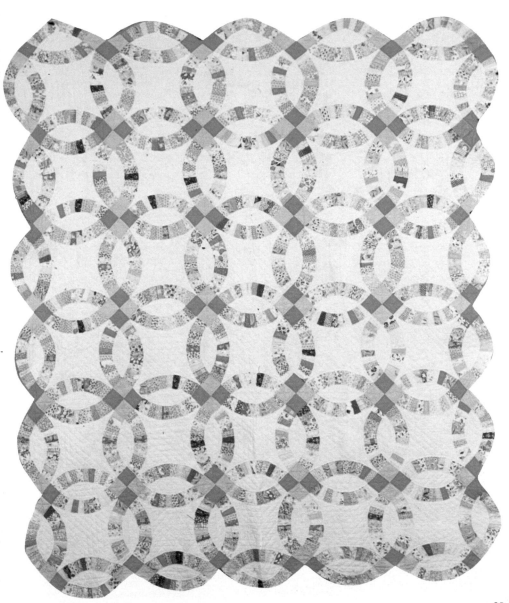

*Traditionally the LOG CABIN pattern represents the roof of a log cabin. The strips of fabric interlocking at the corners are arranged round a central square, often of red fabric, which represents the chimney. The light-coloured part of the block is said to represent the firelight and the dark section the shadows.*

*Log Cabin variations are many. The size of the basic block can be changed by varying the width of the strips and also the size of the central square. As with most forms of pieced work, once the basic blocks have been made they can be arranged to form a number of interesting patterns.*

*Log Cabin quilts became especially popular after the American Civil War.*

**Log Cabin**
**Quilt**
Square: 80 in  203 cm

One of the many versions of the Log Cabin pattern is made from English printed dress cottons. The cotton backing is white with a pink sprig. If this quilt is studied carefully several patterns can be seen in it.

*c.* 1860

**Log Cabin – Straight**
**Furrow Quilt**
L. 84 in 213 cm
W. 72 in 183 cm
*Gift of Mrs H. Dunscombe Colt*

Here the Log Cabin blocks are on a very large scale and have been arranged in the 'Straight furrow' pattern. The colouring is vivid on the top but a more sombre maroon and white printed cotton has been used for the backing.

Late nineteenth century

**Log Cabin – Barn Raising Quilt**
L. 80 in   203 cm
W. 76 in   193 cm
*Gift of Mrs Olive M. Cotterell*

Narrow strips about one half-inch wide have been used for the basic blocks, which have been arranged to form the Barn Raising or Sunshine and Shadow pattern. The top of the quilt was made by Ellen Bryant Smith for her marriage in 1863 in Londonderry, Vermont. Instead of the more usual inferior material for the backing this quilt has what is virtually another top on the reverse.

**Log Cabin – Barn Raising
Reverse of Quilt**

Tiny triangles pieced together to form squares, some only three-quarters of an inch across, which in turn form larger squares in a kaleidoscope of colour, make up the reverse of the Barn Raising quilt. This side was made by Ellen Bryant's sister Sarah Bryant of Mount Holly, Vermont, about 1886.

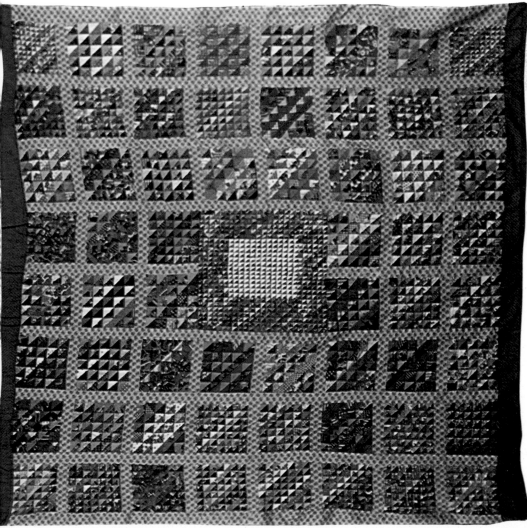

**Log Cabin**
Square: 66 in    168 cm
*Gift of Mrs Wm J. Tyne and*
*Mrs Edward J. Murray Jr*

One-half of each block has been pieced in black silk so that when the blocks were set together a black star alternated with a coloured one. There is no quilting, so probably this piece of needlework was used as a sofa 'throw'. It was made sometime between 1850 and 1900 by Mrs H. A. Batchelor, a Scotswoman living in Michigan, who was grandmother of the donors.

**Log Cabin – Pineapple**
Square: 65 in    165 cm
*Gift of Mrs Timothy E. Ryan*

An intricate version of the Log Cabin block known as 'Pineapple' has been used for this decorative 'throw'. The fabrics are rich – silks, velvets, brocades and tie silks. It was made by Miss Grace Brewster Cross of Chicago, eighth-generation descendant of Elder Brewster, who went to America on the *Mayflower*.

Late nineteenth century

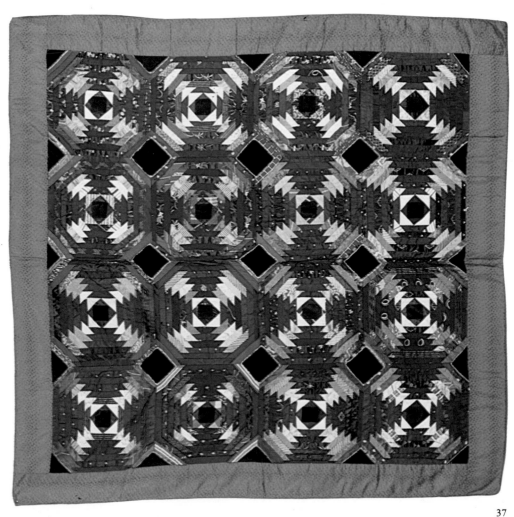

**Darts of Death or
Widow's Quilt**
L. 92 in   234 cm
W. 59 in   150 cm

The pieced blocks of the 'Darts of Death' alternate with plain
white blocks quilted with a harp pattern. The black geometric
shapes representing the darts of death probably came from a
similar pre-Revolutionary pattern known as 'Hosanna' or 'The
Palm'. The name was taken from the story of Jesus' last journey
into Jerusalem when He was saluted with palms and cries of
'Hosanna'. This is the only quilt in the Museum's collection which
is single bed size.

Nineteenth century

**Robbing Peter to Pay Paul Quilt**
L. 81 in    206 cm
W. 85 in    215 cm
*Gift of Mr Howard D. Washburn*

An eye-catching pattern which is simple to make once the basic block has been mastered. A sector is cut from the white block and added to the red. Likewise the sector cut from the red block is added to the white. The skill lies in turning the block through ninety degrees to ensure the continuance of the pattern. This particular pattern is also known as 'Rocky Road to California', 'Drunkard's Path', and 'Country Husband'. A similar block arranged differently is known as 'Steeple Chase' or 'Bows and Arrows'.

As the nineteenth century progressed more attention was paid to the pieced and applique designs than to the quilting and here the quilting is of the simplest – it outlines the shapes.

This quilt was made by the ladies of the Congregational Church, Oriskany Falls, New York, for Mrs Patty (Armour) Washburn and has been signed by the makers. The date 1886 is written on one of the blocks.

*The AMÍSH or Plain People belong to the most conservative sect of the Mennonite Church. Almost all forms of decoration are prohibited, but as quilts are utilitarian objects colours are allowed, although it is essential that the fabrics are of solid colours, no prints being allowed. The quilts are usually made of woollen cloth in the same sombre colours as the clothing worn by the community and often in unusual colour combinations. There is often a small piece of brilliant contrast fabric. Very fine stitching is characteristic of all Amish quilts. The patterns are simple and always geometric, using variations of the diamond, square and triangle.*

**Bars
Quilt**
L. 79 in  201 cm
W. 70 in  178 cm

Very fine woollen fabric has been chosen to make the top of the quilt, which has a cotton backing. As with all Amish quilts the stitching is very well executed.

Lancaster, Pennsylvania
c. 1880

**Churn Dash
Quilt**
L. 80 in   203 cm
W. 70 in   178 cm

As Amish quilt patterns were simple and non-representative, it is unlikely that this pattern would have been called Churn Dash or Monkey Wrench, names by which it is known in non-Amish communities.

The colours are very typical of those used in mid-west Amish quilts and unusually this quilt is made of cotton.

Millersburgh, Ohio
Late nineteenth century

**Floating Bars
Quilt**
L. 88 in   224 cm
W. 75 in   191 cm

The use of deep lavender blue cotton for the border is typical of those Amish quilts made in Ohio. The pattern is known as Floating Bars, as there is no contrasting square in each of the four corners as in the quilt from Pennyslvania. The backing is of grey alpaca and the quilting neat and even.

Ohio
*c.* 1900

Quilts made by the PENNSYLVANIA GERMAN *women are different from those made in other parts of the American continent. Settlers from Germany and eastern Europe brought with them a peasant love of strong colour, as well as patterns which can be traced back to a mediaeval mid-European culture. These people set their own cultural standards, but because of lack of time and money tended to simplify designs and adapt them to American materials. As a consequence the quilts have a distinct character of their own.*

*Some of the finest Pennsylvania German quilts were made between 1800 and 1850.*

**Mariner's Compass Quilt**
Square: 103 in   264 cm
*Gift of Mr George G. Frelinghuysen*

Bold colours have been used in this design. The compass motifs and the sawtooth borders are pieced but the border, like many others, is applique. The materials used are mainly those of the 1820s and 1830s but at some time this quilt was remade – most probably 1840/1850. Fabric was hard to come by and thrifty housewives often remade their quilts.

Pennsylvania

44

*The* COMPASS *motif is one of the most popular in use for Pennsylvania German quilts. Great skill was needed to design the points of the compass in days when mathematics was not a subject taught to young ladies. The central star was formed by folding and refolding a square of fabric. The remaining points would be made in the same way.*

**Compass Star Quilt**
L. 84 in  214 cm
W. 82 in  208 cm

Typical Pennsylvania German Compass Star motifs are pieced. The same fabrics have been used for the dainty shell pattern in the border. The quilting is very complex and has been executed in fine, even stitching.

Pennsylvania
1824

*Patterns using* DIAMONDS *range from the large symmetrical star designs which cover the whole quilt top to blocks incorporating small stars or flowers made from diamonds and triangles. The word 'star' appears in many pattern names and the stars are usually six- or eight-pointed.*

**Sunburst
Quilt**
L. 72 in   183 cm
W. 65 in   165 cm
*Gift of Mrs G. W. Bacon,
grand-daughter of the maker*

Beautifully shaded paisley prints make this large sunburst pattern. The yellow sateen background is quilted in a running feather pattern using red sewing cotton. The backing is of red cotton.

Made in St Cloud, Minnesota, between 1875 and 1900 by Mrs Henry Mitchell (Elizabeth).

**Star Burst
Quilt**
L. 78 in    199 cm
W. 64 in    164 cm
*Gift of Miss Dorothy Dignam*

The large star pieced by sewing machine has been made of diamond shapes cut from cotton fabrics in crude colours. In complete contrast is the backing of white fleecy material printed with dainty floral motifs. The quilting is very simple with rather large stitches. The quilt was made in 1973 by an Indian woman from the Wounded Knee Trading Post.

Indian women have no tradition of sewing with needle and thread, but contact with white women has meant that some have learnt new techniques. However, the patchwork design shows the bold colours and the sharp angular outlines that are traditional with the Indian.

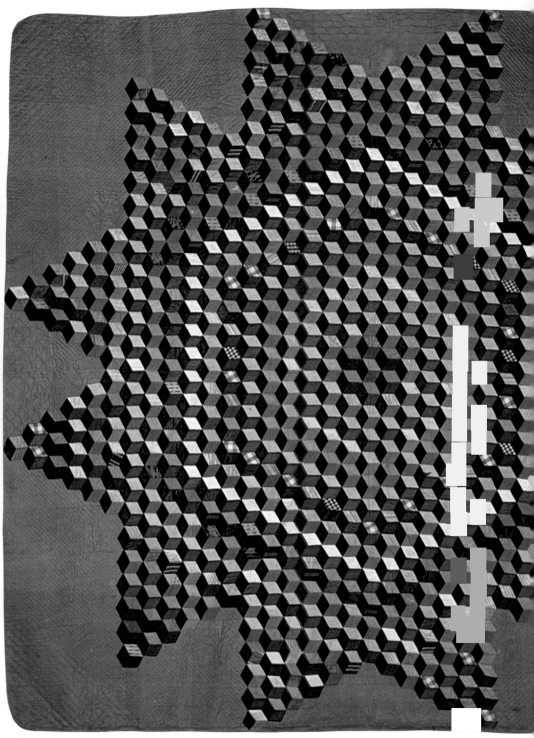

**Tumbling Blocks
Quilt**
Square: 103 in   255 cm
*Gift of Miss Mary
Middleton Rogers,
grand-daughter of the
maker*

**Tumbling Blocks
Quilt**
Square: 103 in   255 cm
*Gift of Miss Mary
Middleton Rogers,
grand-daughter of the
maker*

Multicoloured silk diamonds pieced to form Tumbling Blocks
pattern in turn form one large star which is surrounded by grey
silk. The backing is of bright blue glazed chintz. Leaf patterns
have been quilted between the points of the star and shell quilting
used for the borders.

This magnificent quilt was made in 1852 by a Quaker, Sarah
Taylor Middleton Rogers of Crosswicks, New Jersey, one of the
earliest women physicians in Philadelphia. At the State Fair in
Trenton, New Jersey, this quilt was awarded a prize of a silver
ladle inscribed 'Premium to S.T.M. for silk quilt, 10th Mo. 1852'.

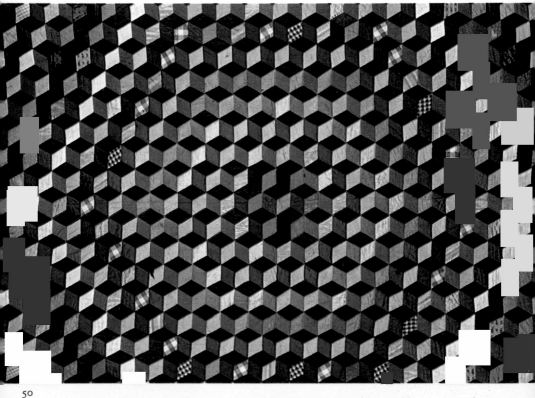

**Ruth Porter's Quilt**
L. 96 in   244 cm
W. 91 in   231 cm

The earliest dated quilt in the Museum's collection bears an inscription 'R... Porter, her bed quilt made in the year 177(7)'? As only the 'R' of the christian name can be deciphered the name Ruth has been given to the maker.

The tiny eight-point stars are pieced and some blocks are embroidered with floral motifs. As with many pieced quilts the border is applique.

**Poinsettia
Quilt**
L.    84 in    213 cm
W.  100 in    254 cm
*Gift of Mr and Mrs
David Stockwell*

Six red diamonds and two green make each flower. Over the years
parts of the red fabric have rotted but have been neatly darned.
The alternate blocks are very finely quilted. Some seeds remain in
the cotton padding.

The Poinsettia (*Euphorbia pulcherrima*) is a Mexican plant and its
name honours Dr J. P. Poinsett, who first exhibited the plant in
Pennsylvania in 1829.

*c.* 1840

**North Carolina Lily Quilt**
Square: 89 in   226 cm

This shape of diamonds with triangles can be used in many different ways and known by different names. It has always been popular. On Long Island the shape makes a pattern known as 'Duck's Foot in the Mud', in Ohio 'Bear's Paw' and in Philadelphia, stronghold of the Society of Friends, 'Hand of Friendship'.

Here the shape has been used to form a lily flower. Known also as the Meadow Lily in New England and Tiger Lily in Pennsylvania, the name changed again to Mountain Lily, Fire Lily, Prairie Lily and Mariposa Lily as the pattern gradually spread westwards.

The alternate white blocks have been quilted with feather circles and floral and leaf patterns.

Nineteenth century

*Mosaic patchwork, using* HEXAGONS *of very small size, was popular in America during the first half of the nineteenth century. Instructions for making 'honeycomb', a type of mosaic patchwork, were published in the February 1835 issue of 'Godey's Lady's Book', a well-known magazine of the time.*

*The hexagons can be arranged in clusters as in the various flower garden patterns, or used in conjunction with diamonds and triangles to make a geometric design.*

**Mosaic Diamonds
Quilt**
L. 105 in   267 cm
W. 100 in   254 cm
*Gift of Nancy, Countess of
Dunraven, grand-daughter of
the maker*

Hexagons made from printed cottons are joined to form diamond shapes. The placing of the diamond-shaped motifs gives a three-dimensional effect to the pattern, similar to Tumbling Blocks. Each hexagon is quilted across, forming six small triangles.

The quilt was made in 1861 by Anne Eliza Urquhart (née Blunt) of Charlie's Hope Plantation, Southampton Co., Virginia. It is very similar to one started about 1830 by Hester Maria Monroe, daughter of President Monroe, and which was never finished.

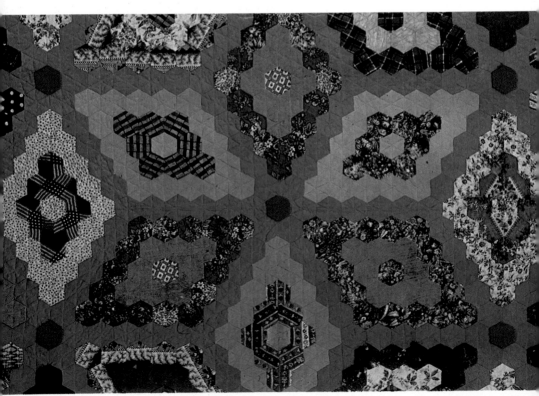

**Grandmother's Flower
Garden
Quilt**
Square: 78 in    198 cm

English furnishing fabrics of the 1820s have been used for the motifs in this very popular design. Each 'flower bed' has been surrounded by a ring of white hexagonal shapes.

The border is English chintz made about 1810.

Not all the hexagons have been cut out individually. In many of the motifs a group of three hexagons have been cut in one piece, thus obviating the need for two centre seams.

Maryland
c. 1840

**Little School Houses Quilt**
L. 81 in  206 cm
W. 62 in  158 cm

During the second half of the nineteenth century one of the most popular patterns was the 'Little School House', normally made with red cottons. This example using blue is unusual. The design is thought to have originated in New Jersey, but this quilt was found in Westerly, Rhode Island.

Late nineteenth century

**Fanny's Fan
Throw**
Square: 62 in 159 cm
*Gift of Mrs Mary Shaw,
niece of the maker*

Fans pieced from rich silks, ribbons and brocades have been applied to dull black satin, and the whole heavily embroidered with great skill. Initials and date 'R B W 1900' have been embroidered in the bottom right corner of the border. A piece of work as elaborate as this would not have been made for a bed but would more likely have been used as a 'throw' for the sofa.

The throw was made in 1900 by Rachel Boone Wintersteen of Port Carbon, Pennsylvania. Rachel, who was a Quaker, wished to marry a man of a different religion but this was not allowed. As a consequence she never married and this coverlet, made for her hope chest, was never used.

# Applique Quilts

In mediaeval times, when textiles were scarce and expensive, pieces of rich woven fabric, too precious to throw away, were used as a substitute for embroidery by being sewn to the surface of another piece of cloth.

This same technique was used for the first applique bedcovers. Floral and bird motifs, often the best pieces left over from worn-out bedhangings, were cut from Indian chintzes and palampores (cotton bedcovers) and applied to a foundation material. The foundation itself often comprised several pieces of fabric joined together. It was usual to cover the back of the chintz cut-outs with some kind of paste in order to keep them firm. When the paste was dry they were laid on the foundation material and sewn round. Subsequent washings removed the paste. This technique was known as 'Broderie Perse'.

The whole concept of applique quilt tops is pictorial. The applique patterns on the top could make up one large design as in a painting, or smaller designs could be executed on blocks which were then joined together in the same way as the pieced work. The designs were often drawn freehand as in the many floral and leaf patterns. In addition abstract patterns could be made by the folded paper cut-out process, which was used to great effect in some of the Hawaiian designs.

In order to give a three-dimensional effect to certain parts of a design, particularly flowers and buds, a padding of fine cotton was inserted beneath the applique shape before it was sewn to the foundation fabric.

It has often been said that pieced quilts were for everyday use and applique quilts were for best, but there seems little evidence to support this. The quiltmaker herself designed her quilt in whichever medium she favoured and made it with whatever materials were available.

**Tiles**
**Top only**
L. 98 in   249 cm
W. 82 in   208 cm
*Gift of Mrs Paul Moore*

Floral and bird motifs as well as countryside scenes have been used for this top. The English chintzes include a copper plate print of the 1770s, a roller print of about 1800 and other fabrics ranging in date from 1810 to 1880. The motifs are in excellent condition and could have been 'samples' saved up over the years.

*c.* 1900

**Tree of Life**
**Quilt**
L. 106 in  269 cm
W. 101 in  257 cm
*Gift of Mrs Giles Whiting*

From advertisements in newspapers which were published on the east coast of America it is known that India 'chinces' and glazed 'chinces' were being imported into the American continent before 1715. As well as yard goods, palampores (cotton bedcovers) were available. These were mordant dyed with details painted in by hand after dyeing. One of the most popular patterns was the 'Tree of Life', a large central tree with exotic flowers and fruit. Birds too were invariably included. When the palampore was worn out the best pieces were cut away to be used again, appliqued to a fine homespun backing, as the top of another bedcover. As in this instance a large pictorial design was often the result. The quilting, which is diagonal throughout, is executed in tiny stitches and is typical of the quilting which was done on many early quilts. Repairs involving the use of several different chintzes can be seen in the border.

Late eighteenth century

**Red Birds**
**Top only**
L.  118 in   284 cm
W.  92 in   234 cm
*Gift of Mrs Paul Moore*

The top consists of twenty blocks of white calico divided by a very narrow green band. Each block contains an applique bird, flowers and foliage, but no two blocks are exactly alike.

The border is an elaborate applique version of the feather pattern.

Mid nineteenth century

*Some of the traditional quilting patterns from the north of England are based on a FEATHER motif, and similar motifs can be found in many places in North America. Here the feathers have been used in an applique pattern.*

**Princess Feather
Quilt**
Square: 79 in   201 cm
*Gift of Mrs L. Boyd Hatch*

The bright colours of the Princess Feather applique contrast with the very finely executed quilting, particularly of the pineapples. A design such as this is called the Princess Feather, as it seems to resemble the feathers in an Indian princess's headdress. Alternatively, the name could be a corruption of Prince's feathers, the fleur-de-lys.

Nineteenth century

**Princess Feather
Quilt**
Square: 102 in    259 cm

A slightly different type of Princess Feather which strongly resembles the 'Welsh Fern' quilting pattern is used for the applique on this rather large quilt. The colouring is bold and the quilting on a larger scale, and more simple than on the previous quilt. Interest is added by the stars between the feather motifs.

The feather patterns on American applique quilts tended to have a serrated edge whilst those in Britain were rounded and smooth.

Nineteenth century

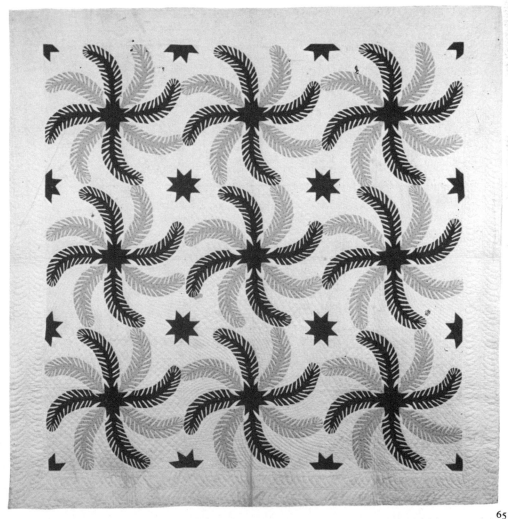

*In the nineteenth century* OAK LEAVES *were the symbol of long life, which no doubt accounts for the number of quilts made with variations of this pattern. Sometimes the name 'Charter Oak' is given to these patterns. The name comes from the historic tree which formerly stood in Hartford, Connecticut. In 1686 Sir Edmund Andros was appointed Governor of New England by James II. When Andros came to reclaim the Connecticut Charter, the candles at the night session of the Assembly were suddenly extinguished and the Charter was saved from seizure by being carried away by Captain Joseph Wadsworth and hidden in the hollow of an ancient tree – the 'Charter Oak'.*

**Oak Leaves Quilt**
L.  100 in  234 cm
W.  94 in  239 cm

Neat applique pattern of green oak leaves with red and green inner pattern known as 'The Reel'. The quilting is intricate with a swirling running feather pattern in the border.

Pennsylvania
1830/50

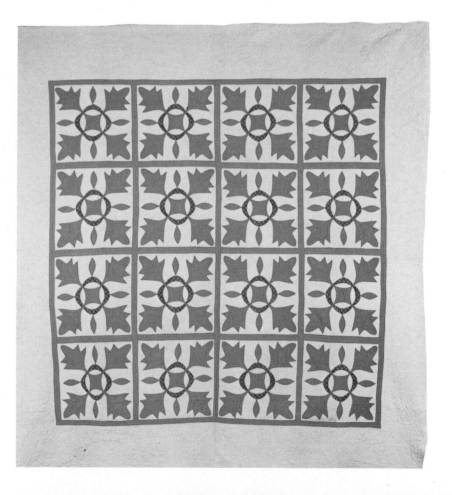

**Oak Leaves
Quilt**
Square: 86 in   218 cm

The design of the block is very similar to that of the preceding quilt, the oak leaves surrounding the reel pattern. In this instance there is an interesting border of triangles made from both white and patterned fabric. The quilting bears no relation to the applique design but is sewn in straight lines in the outline of the log cabin pattern.

It has been suggested that the reel represented one of the everyday tasks of most women – spinning. The reel was used to wind the yarn into skeins.

Mid nineteenth century

**Red Calicoes
Quilt**
Square: 81 in    205 cm

The brilliant red colour, practically fast to washing, known as Turkey Red was introduced into England from the east in the eighteenth century and into America about 1829. Prior to this time all red shades had been obtained from the madder plant.

This cottage type quilt in which different patterned red calicoes have been used for each block shows some interesting variations on the use of red and white.

The applique pattern has been cut with great precision. A square of fabric was folded in half lengthwise, then across and then diagonally and a pattern cut round two sides of the resulting triangle. When the cloth was unfolded a symmetrical pattern had been formed which was then sewn to the foundation block. The quilting is simple but well done.

Berks County, Pennsylvania
Mid nineteenth century

**Quilt**
L. 75 in   191 cm
W. 70 in   178 cm
*Gift of Mrs A. Davies,*
*grand-daughter of the maker*

Here the applique patterns must surely have been cut direct from the cloth without the help of a paper pattern. No two blocks are quite the same. The frill has been added by sewing machine at a later date. The use of blue and white fabrics give a fresh and sparkling look to the quilt.

Made by Anne Edwards from Wales, who emigrated to America with her husband.

*c.* 1870

*Before woven cloth was introduced into the* HAWAIIAN *Islands clothes were made from 'tapa', a kind of pounded bark which was felted into the correct shape and needed no sewing. The wives of New England missionaries brought their scrap bags with them to the islands and taught the native women how to sew and to make patchwork. It is not known just when the traditional patchwork patterns were superseded by the 'all over' applique patterns used today. These quilts are made of whole cloth, rarely of more than two colours, using a folded paper 'cut-out' technique resulting in a symmetrical pattern radiating from the centre. The border, maile lei, is made in the same way. Patterns are symbolic and recur frequently in different combinations. The older Hawaiian 'kapa' bedcovers have simpler designs, many of which were taken from the fruits and foliage of the islands.*

**Quilt**
L. 94 in    239 cm
W. 84 in    213 cm
*Gift of Mrs Murray Ward*

A striking example of the Hawaiian whole cloth applique. The quilt is thickly padded.

Twentieth century

**Quilt**
L. 83 in 211 cm
W. 75 in 191
*Gift of Mr George G.*
*Frelinghuysen*

The theme of this Hawaiian quilt is a formalised design representing Queen Kapiolani's fan and Kahilis cut from red cotton and appliqued to the white cotton background. The Maile lei (border) is also applied. The quilting follows the outline of the patterns in rows one half-inch apart, rather like the contour lines on a map, hence its name – contour quilting. The padding is very thick.

Twentieth century

**Hawaiian Flag
Quilt**
L. 80 in   203 cm
W. 70 in   178 cm
*Gift of Mr George G.
Frelinghuysen*

In 1794, Captain George Vancouver, who had been a junior officer
when Captain Cook discovered the Hawaiian Islands in 1778,
presented the British flag to King Kamehameha the Great. The
King was suitably impressed with the honour and accepted British
protection. For twenty-two years the British flag was used as the
actual flag of the Hawaiian kingdom.

By 1816 it was felt that Hawaii should have a flag of her own.
With the help of many advisers, including it is thought two friendly
British sea captains, a new flag was designed. This showed eight
horizontal stripes in white, red and blue, representing the eight
inhabited islands of the group, with the Union Jack at the head
to signify the King's respect for Britain.

For eighty-two years, with one brief interval, this flag proudly
proclaimed Hawaiian nationality. The interval occurred in 1893,
when for a period of two months, the national flag was replaced
by that of the United States of America as the result of local
unrest. This became an occasion of such profound sorrow that the
islands were swept by a wave of patriotism and many Hawaiian
ladies retired to their homes to make flag patterned quilts. This is
one of them.

On the occasion of the annexation of the islands in 1898, the
flag was finally lowered amid scenes of deep emotion. It continued
its existence as the territorial flag and then, when President
Eisenhower signed the Bill granting statehood on 18th March,
1959, it took on a new lease of life as the State flag.

*c.* 1893

*From the time the TULIP was introduced into Europe in the sixteenth century and thence to America, it became a favourite flower. It was accepted in Germany as a variation of the Holy Lily, the three flowers symbolising the Trinity. The tulip motif is widely used on Pennsylvania German quilts. It has a simple outline which even an inexperienced needlewoman could manage.*

**Tulips and Ribbons Quilt**
L. 87 in   221 cm
W. 83 in   210 cm

The zig-zag border contrasts sharply with the curves of the applique tulips and ribbons. The vivid colours are typical of those used for Pennsylvania German quilts.

Pennsylvania
*c.* 1840/50

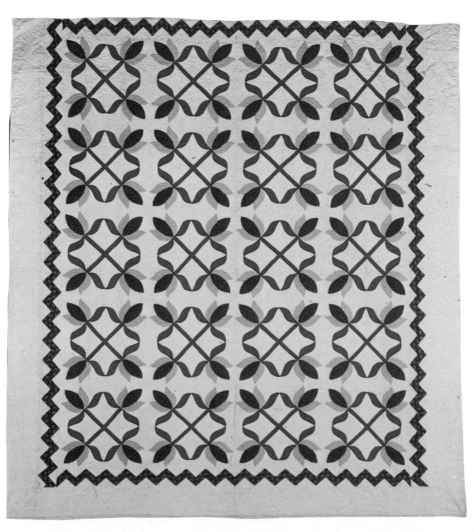

*The* PINEAPPLE, *widely used both as an applique pattern and a quilting pattern, is a native of South America. The first pineapple sent to England was presented to Oliver Cromwell in 1657, and John Evelyn mentions in his diary that he had seen the famous 'Queen Pine'. Pineapples soon became a passion and were used as a decoration on objects as diverse as teapots and gateposts. Reference was made to pineapples in literature also. Mrs Malaprop in Sheridan's play 'The Rivals' refers to 'the pineapple of politeness', meaning the height of politeness.*

**Pineapples**
**Quilt**
L. 99 in   252 cm
W. 77 in   196 cm
*Gift of Miss Dorothy Weston*

The neat 'swags and bow-knots' applique border enhances the pineapple motif. This is another quilt where the cotton seeds remain in the padding.

Made about 1850 by Leila Adams Weston, possibly in Pennsylvania.

**Pennsylvania Pineapple Quilt**
Square: 88 in 224 cm
*Gift of Mrs Monroe Hewlett*

Applique pineapples form the main theme, but Meadow Lily and Tulip patterns appear in the corner blocks. One pineapple block is appliqued in a different colour from the others – perhaps the maker's deliberate mistake. Many needlewomen followed the eastern belief that God alone could create a perfect piece of work. Consequently they made a deliberate mistake so as not to incur His wrath.

In the lower left-hand block is written in indelible ink 'Harriet C. Wade Remember Me'.

The quilt was in the trousseau of Amelia Mellick of Light Stree near Bloomsburg, Pennsylvania, maternal grandmother of the done

Nineteenth century

*The* ROSE OF SHARON, *always a popular pattern particularly for brides' quilts, has romantic associations. The name comes from the Song of Solomon—'Let him kiss me with the kisses of his mouth. For thy love is better than wine. I am the Rose of Sharon and the Lily of the Valleys ...'*

**Rose of Sharon**
**Quilt**
Square: 96 in   219 cm
*Gift of Mrs Monroe Hewlett*

The Rose of Sharon pattern has been neatly contained within the block. The quilting in diagonal lines is in small, even stitches, characteristic of the Pennsylvania needlewoman.

This quilt was in the trousseau of Amelia Mellick, a Quaker, of Light Street, near Bloomsburg, Pennsylvania, maternal grandmother of the donor.

Mid nineteenth century

**Rose of Sharon Quilt**

L. 98 in   249 cm
W. 80 in   203 cm

The flowers and buds of the Roses of Sharon are stuffed slightly to give them more prominence. The quilting incorporates flowers and leaves with hearts.

The quilt was made by Lavinia Krishner of New York, in 1850. Her daughter embroidered her mother's initials and those of her father, John Fox, and the date of her parents' marriage, 1850, in the border. John Fox was taken by the Indians as a baby and given the name Little Fox. Being ignorant of his real name later in life he called himself John Fox.

**Quilt**
L. 99 in   250 cm
W. 79 in   201 cm
*Gift of Mrs Nancy Lancaster*

Quilts such as this, made of homespun woollen materials, are rare. It was probably a bride's quilt, as the motifs include a heart, lilies of the valley and the Rose of Sharon. The inspiration for the pattern seems to have been religious, but the circles and other geometric shapes which enclose some of the patterns could be masonic motifs. Other symbolic motifs include pansies for thoughts, pomegranates for fruitfulness and vines for plenty.

The quilt has obviously been much used as the original backing has worn out, as has a second backing. The present backing, the third, is modern.

New England
1830/40

An ALBUM QUILT *was a co-operative effort. Each of the many squares was made by a different individual who wished to honour the person to whom the quilt was to be presented. The squares, often signed and dated, included motifs relevant to the recipient's life or interests. Scripture quilts included passages from the Bible and Brides' quilts always included hearts. A Friendship quilt was often made by members of a Church and presented to one of its members or to the Minister. A Freedom quilt was made for a young man by the girls of his acquaintance on his reaching the age of twenty-one. It would then be put away until he gave it as his gift to the hope chest of his future bride.*

*Album quilts were also made for hospital use. Weldon's 'Practical Patchwork', published about 1900, tells us that 'Hospital quilts are made of good sized squares of red twill and white calico placed alternately like squares on a chess board, the white pieces having texts written on them or scripture pictures outlined in marking ink; they are much appreciated and prove a great source of interest to the poor invalids.'*

**Album Quilt Top**
Square: 69 in   175 cm

The date 1862 on this top, which was never made up into a quilt, indicates that it was put together during the Civil War, possibly in memory of someone who had died. Several of the texts illustrate the theme of sleep – but sleep meaning death. The twenty-third Psalm is written out in full and the text under the crossed flags reads 'He giveth his beloved sleep.'

Newark, New Jersey

**The Baltimore Bride
Quilt**
Square: 122 in    314 cm
*Gift of Mr Frank T. Howard*

## The Baltimore Bride Quilt

Square: 122 in   314 cm
*Gift of Mr Frank T. Howard*

Obviously made for a large double bed this album quilt is of a type which was especially popular in the Baltimore area, and since many of the best examples have been found there they are often referred to as Baltimore Brides' quilts.

Because of the similarity of some of the designs it is possible that some blocks were made from a professionally drawn pattern or were bought in 'kit' form. The hearts on this quilt are geometric and can be seen at the end of each horizontal banding strip.

A number of the blocks have been signed and on one has been inscribed in indelible ink, a poem and the signature 'Alice A. Ryder, April 1st, 1847, Baltimore, Md.'

**Christmas Bride Quilt**
Square: 74 in 188 cm

The heart shapes and holly leaves have been made from cotton which was originally green but which has now faded to beige. The berries are slightly padded. The quilting is intricate, using feather circles, running feather and floral patterns. The applique border is very similar to others in the collection. It was considered unlucky to put hearts on anything but a Bride's quilt, so that it is possible that this particular bride was married at Christmas.

Nineteenth century

84

**Mrs Waterbury**
**Album Quilt**
L. 95 in  241 cm
W. 84 in  213 cm
*Gift of Mrs Hassel Smith*

The centre block of the quilt states that it was made for the Rev. Mrs Waterbury by her friends and presented on 1st April, 1853. The patterns, which have been well co-ordinated, include pictures of the Bible, Psalms and tombstones, as well as simple applique patterns. It is interesting to see the variation of the swastika which originally was considered a mystic symbol and is common to both eastern and western peoples. It is a symbol of motion, but also means good fortune, health and long life and no doubt it was for that reason included in the patterns on this quilt. Many of the blocks have been signed, some singly, some by groups of people, and some of the signatories are men.

New Jersey

## Bicentennial Friendship Quilt

L.  106 in  269 cm
W.   93 in  213 cm

Made by staff of the American Museum in Britain and some of their American friends, this Bicentennial Friendship quilt incorporates blocks from many parts of the United States of America. The crossed flags in the centre block are symbolic of the friendship which exists between the two countries. Each participant chose her own design, and in many instances the applique pattern on the block represents an object from the Museum's collection and is indicative of the room in which the maker usually works. The quilt is backed with white cotton, bearing a green floral motif which matches the green of the banding. The quilting is very simple.

A quilt where each block contains a different pattern is known as a Friendship Medley quilt.

1975/76

**Flowers for Friendship Quilt**

L. 100 in   254 cm
W. 80 in   236 cm

Also made by the staff of the American Museum in Britain, this quilt designed by Barbara Meru Frears incorporates the floral emblems of the thirteen original States with quilted feather circles in the centre panel. The border consists of the emblems of England – Rose, Scotland – Thistle, Wales – Daffodil and Leek, and Ireland – Shamrock. The panel at the foot shows an eagle with the dates 1776 and 1976.

The Mayflower is the emblem of Massachusetts, Connecticut and Pennsylvania share the Mountain Laurel, New Hampshire the Purple Lilac, while the Violet is the emblem of both Rhode Island and New Jersey. New York has a yellow Rose and Georgia the Cherokee Rose, Delaware the Peach Blossom and Maryland the Black-eyed Susan. Virginia and North Carolina share the Dogwood, whilst South Carolina has the Carolina Jasmine as an emblem.

1975/76

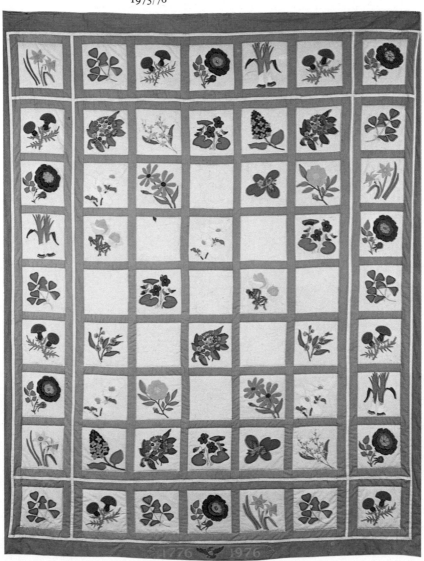

**Cartoon**
**Coverlet**
L. 79 in  201 cm
W. 76 in  196 cm
*Gift of Mrs Margaret Jackson*

The figures in the comic scenes illustrated here are all to scale and the clothing most realistic. Each picture has a comic caption, no doubt illustrating the type of humour which was common about the middle of the nineteenth century. One scene shows a tramp and the caption reads 'Well if my boots do let the vater in at the toes they lets it out at the heels.' One caption which seems particularly appropriate at the present time asks 'Lor love you, sonny, why don't your mother cut your hair?' The coverlet is not padded.

The coverlet was made in Saratoga, New York, in the middle of the nineteenth century by Mrs Peter Porter (Martha Vail) Wiggins.

**Garden Wreath
Quilt**
L. 87 in   221 cm
W. 71 in   180 cm

Applique versions of Rose Wreath, Rose of Sharon and other floral motifs alternate with blocks containing green leaves which have been pieced. The applique border is a variation of the wandering tulip pattern.

Nineteenth century.

90

**Turkey Tracks**
L. 94 in  239 cm
W. 80 in  203 cm

Fabric of unusual colouring has been used for the 'Turkey Tracks' design. The alternate white blocks are quilted very finely and with great expertise in a wandering vine pattern, which meanders from block to block across the whole quilt.

Originally this pattern and its variations was called 'Wandering Foot', and it was said that whoever slept under it would always have the wanderlust. No bride would ever have a 'Wandering Foot' patterned quilt in her hope chest. Because of its unhappy associations the name was changed to 'Turkey Tracks', which seemed to break the spell as it became a very popular pattern.

Maryland
c. 1840/50

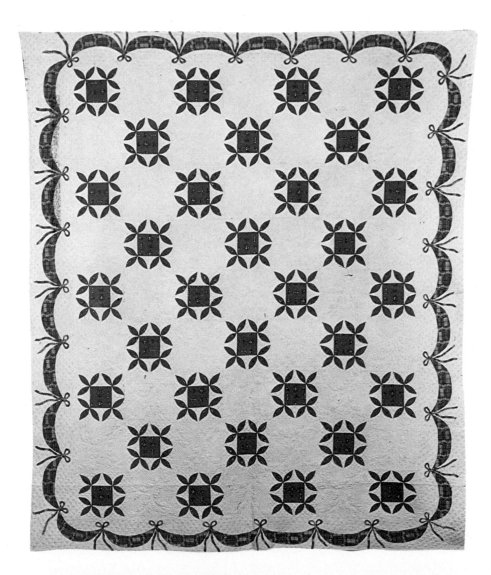

**Ohio Farmyard Quilt**

Square: 85 in    216 cm

The name Adela E. Dimling has been embroidered on to the central block. This quilt with its pattern of horses, rosebuds and cockscombs surely suggests the sights and sounds of Adela's Ohio farm yard.

Nineteenth century

**Children's Menagerie Quilt**
L. 74 in   188 cm
W. 62 in   158 cm

Animals and birds have always been popular subjects for needlework and here the shapes have been cut from printed and solid coloured cottons and appliqued to the block. Embroidery highlights the details. Machine stitching has been used in places.

This has obviously been a much-loved quilt as the top and bottom are almost threadbare.

*c.* 1900

# The Quilting Frame

The basic quilting frame consists of two long wooden bars called rails and two shorter flat pieces of wood called stretchers. The stretchers fit into slots in the rails and are held in place by wooden pegs. Each rail has a piece of braid or webbing attached to its inner edge.

Generally, each end of this frame would rest on the top of a straight-backed chair so that the frame could be easily stowed away when sewing for the day was finished. Sometimes the frame rested on trestles, and in the mountain areas of eastern Kentucky and eastern Tennessee, a frame, the full size of the quilt, is lowered from the ceiling by rope and pulley when quilting is to begin. At the end of the day the quilt is hauled up to the ceiling once again.

The quilting frame in the Museum's collection is unusual in that the trestles on which it stands are an integral part of the frame. Ratchets at one end hold the quilt firmly in place. Quilting frames of this type are very rare.

If the quilting is to be done by a number of women then a square frame with a trestle at each corner is often used. The whole quilt can then be put in the frame, and as the work progresses the trestles can be moved in and the quilt rolled on to make the centre of the work more accessible.

The method of working is the same whichever type of frame is used. The three layers are tacked together then all three layers are tacked to the webbing on the rails and are rolled on together, leaving a piece of fabric about two feet wide on which to sew. As the work progresses the quilt is wound on to the front rail, thus exposing an unsewn stretch of fabric.

Quilting is the last process in the making of a quilt, tying together the applique or pieced top, the filling and the backing with a design sewn in running stich.

# Crazy Patchwork

In Colonial days 'crazy' patchwork using humble materials put to good use scraps of fabric regardless of size, shape or colour. By the second half of the nineteenth century crazy patchwork was very ornate, being made from silks, satins, brocades and velvets heavily embellished with embroidery stitches, many of which cannot be found in any embroidery book but were original to the individual needlewoman. Flowers and birds painted on silk were often included as well as ribbon embroidery, chenille work and photographs.

Many crazy quilts were not bedcovers at all but were used as 'throws' to grace the arm of a sofa or perhaps a piano. Crazy patchwork was used to make items other than quilts or throws – mats for the dressing table or mantelshelf, cushion covers and even portières.

Although a 'kit' to make crazy patchwork was advertised in *Godey's Lady's Book* as early as 1855, this type of needlework did not reach the height of its popularity until after 1870.

**Crazy 'Throw'**
Square: 66 in    169 cm
*Gift of Miss Elizabeth McCance*

A crazy 'throw' made in blocks, each block bearing the name of a member of the McCance family – Mother, Bertie, Virginia, Minnie and so on. The arrangement of the pieces of fabric is much more orderly than on most crazy throws and the embroidery is very neat. Originally feather stitch was used on this type of throw to cover the raw edges of the scraps of fabric, but gradually the throws became an excuse to show off more and more embroidery stitches. Flowers and birds have been embroidered on some of the fabrics as well as the date – 1883.

The throw is backed with maroon sateen and has a border of the same fabric. It is not quilted but is tied or knotted.

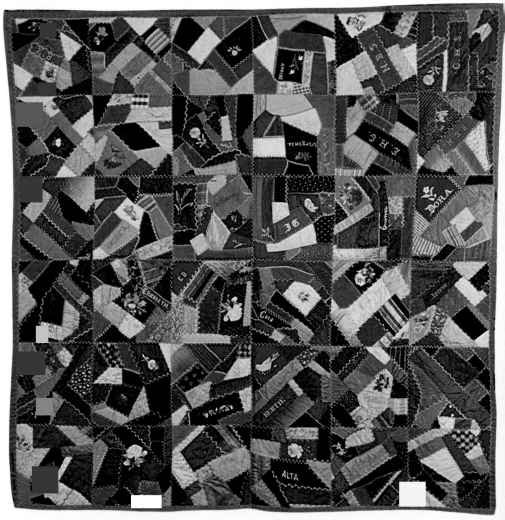

96

**Crazy 'Throw'**
L. 71 in  180 cm
W. 57 in  145 cm
*Gift of Mrs A. A. Williams*

This sofa throw is bordered with plum-coloured velvet which at the top has been embroidered in fine chenille. Several photographs have been incorporated into the design and the horseshoe and initials in the centre could mean that this was made for a hope chest or perhaps as a wedding present.

At the bottom a horse's head and $100 have been embroidered. Perhaps the maker was commemorating a profitable day at the races.

Late nineteenth century

**Portière**
L. 72 in    183 cm
W. 47 in    119 cm
*Gift of Mrs Grace R. Bedenkapp*

One of a pair of door curtains made by Saedia Smith Johnson
(1886–1958), the donor's mother. They were made while she was
living in Manitoba, where the lack of social life inspired this
elaborate work. Mrs Bedenkapp remembers these curtains being in
use all her life. In the top left corner is embroidered the date Jan.
24th 1887 while in the lower left corner appears the inscription
'Finis August 1890'. It is uncertain whether these dates apply to the
pair of curtains or this one only. Note the spider's web made from
the 'eyes' of hooks and eyes, the fan, the numerous animals and
birds and the richness of the fabrics and embroidery.

# Candlewick Coverlets

During the early part of the nineteenth century many American women used a cotton 'roving', an inexpensive type of twisted cotton, for embroidery, or as part of the woven pattern on coverlets. The roving was similar to that which was used for making the wicks of candles. These spreads were not made for warmth but were purely decorative

Some spreads made of linen or cotton twill were embroidered with a design in a light-weight roving, a heavier cord being used for the laid and couched work. The couching was not drawn through the cloth but was formed into a braid which was then sewn to the surface of the work. This type of embroidery stemmed from the seventeenth- and early eighteenth-century English work where bedspreads of twilled linen were embroidered with a fine white cord, laid and couched.

Patterns tended to be similar, with a large vase or basket in the centre and flowers, foliage and fruit arranged to hide the seams, where several pieces of cloth had been joined to form the required width. Similar floral motifs were arranged at each corner.

Other candlewick coverlets were tufted. The wicking was drawn through the background material, using large running stitches which were raised over a twig. When the twig was removed and the wicking had been sheared to leave short ends the spread was washed. Shrinkage of the foundation fabric anchored the strands of roving and the cut ends fluffed out to make a small 'pom pom'.

Candlewicking was used in woven coverlets which had a fine cotton warp and weft. This technique did not originate in America but seems to derive from the white coverlets woven first in Bolton, Lancashire, and then in Canada. About 1820 this type of coverlet began to be made in the United States of America but it is very difficult to differentiate between the British, Canadian and American spreads.

The raised pattern for these spreads was made by the weaver picking up with a piece of stick or a wire certain loops of the roving from the flat weaving. The sticks or wires could be of different diameters to obtain different thicknesses and the loops could be cut if a fluffy effect was desired. The patterns of the woven candlewick bedspreads were often geometric, sometimes resembling the designs of patchwork quilts.

**Coverlet**
Square: 97 in   246 cm

An all-white coverlet made from three pieces of home-woven cotton twill joined together has been embroidered with a cotton roving. It has a typical pattern of a vase of flowers in the centre with floral motifs in the corners. The embroidery is mainly couched candlewicking and the grapes have been executed in a raised cross stitch. At the top can be seen the initials 'V.B.' and the date 1818.

Pennsylvania

**Mary Young's Coverlet**
L. 104 in  264 cm
W. 102 in  259 cm

This coverlet also has been made from three pieces of fabric joined together. The weaving is well executed and the name and date have been woven into the centre panel. The remainder of the pattern is geometric. The roving used for the pattern is very fine. A wide and rather elaborate cotton fringe has been added on three sides.

1821

**Coverlet**
L. 88 in    224 cm
W. 81 in    206 cm
*Gift of Mrs Harrison D. Colt*

A professionally woven coverlet without seams. The pattern is very similar in tradition to those which were woven at Bolton in Lancashire. The letters 'RBSF 10' appear in the lower left corner.

From Ridgefield, Connecticut
1810

# Woven Coverlets

Despite the early establishment of a textile factory at Rowley in Massachusetts, weaving remained largely a cottage industry until after the War of Independence. The need to establish a textile industry was fully appreciated, but at a time when manufactured goods were not easily available and warm bedcovers were a necessity most women made their own, whether quilted or woven.

The oldest woven coverlets had a homespun linen warp, but when cotton became a staple crop it was substituted for linen. Dyes did not 'take' so well on linen as on wool, so invariably the warp was of natural linen or cotton and the weft of indigo or madder dyed wool.

All women were taught to weave simple patterns in the home. For the more complicated patterns, however, the home weaver usually needed skilled assistance. The patterns, called 'drafts', were narrow strips of paper recording a series of straight lines, dots and dashes – the codes by which the design was woven. The drafts were kept rolled and traditionally were tied with black thread.

The simple overshot weave was most generally used and, due to the limitations of the loom, patterns were always geometric. After 1820, when the Jacquard attachment reached America, more elaborate designs could be woven and patterns underwent a radical change. Also about this time large numbers of skilled weavers emigrated from Scandinavia, Germany and Scotland. After working in the east for some time many moved further west, particularly to Ohio, Indiana, Illinois and Iowa. These Jacquard weavers were professionals and the weaver would incorporate his name or initials, the date, often the name of a town, and sometimes the name of the person for whom the coverlet had been woven, into his piece of work. Many patterns woven professionally on Jacquard looms are very similar – roses, lilies and sunbursts in particular.

For about one hundred years from the 1720s the double weave was popular, particularly in Pennsylvania, where settlers from Europe had brought patterns with them. As double weave coverlets have two sets of warp threads and two wefts which are joined at intervals, they used a great deal of yarn and are slow to weave, so they were rarely to be found in the more remote regions.

The great years of coverlet weaving ended with the Civil War, after which factory-made blankets became cheap and plentiful. Old spinning and weaving skills began to die out but the original methods of production remained in general use in the south, particularly in the isolated areas of Tennessee and Kentucky, far longer than they did in the north. While traditionally made coverlets were still being woven in Kentucky until the 1930s, a similar product from New England would have had to have been made earlier than 1830, because by that time much textile production had already been taken over by machinery.

**Woven Coverlet**
**Amanda**
L. 94 in    239 cm
W. 72 in    183 cm

This home-produced coverlet has been woven in a twill weave from natural and indigo dyed wools. The stars and the name and date at the top 'Amanda Wright 1845' have been embroidered in indigo dyed wool. The coverlet was woven in two pieces and has been seamed down the middle and a fringe has been added to three sides.

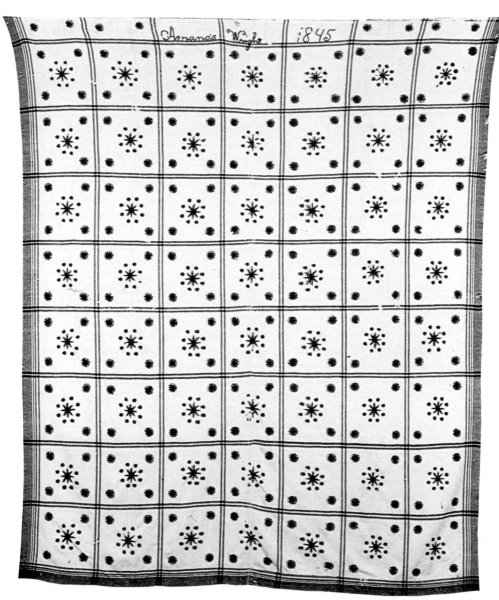

**Woven Coverlet**
L. 83 in   211 cm
W. 81 in   206 cm

Overshot weave coverlet with a natural cotton warp and blue and gold wool weft woven in two sections and joined. The lower corners have been cut away so that it would fit neatly round the posts of a four-poster bed.

Early nineteenth century

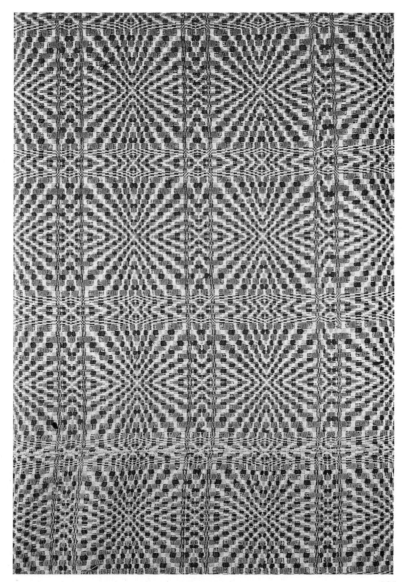

**Pinecone Bloom
Woven Coverlet**
L. 100 in   254 cm
W. 81 in   206 cm
*Gift of the late Mr Eric D.
Remington*

Finely woven in three widths with a natural cotton warp and an indigo wool weft, by Lucinda Ann Wright (1825–1918) of Paris, Kentucky, grandmother of the donor. Mid nineteenth century.

Another coverlet in the Museum's collection woven about 1900 in the same pattern by Nancy Laura McWilliam, mother of the donor, has a natural cotton warp and a cream wool weft.

**Woven Coverlet**
L. 86 in  218 cm
W. 83 in  211 cm

The only woven coverlet in the Museum's collection which has green in it has been woven from natural cotton and indigo, red and green wools. This type of coverlet could have been woven either on a power loom or on a hand loom complete with a Jacquard attachment.

Jacquard's invention used a punched card system which enabled groups of warp threads to be raised or lowered according to the pattern. The punched cards were held on a continuous roll above the loom, and some of the wires on a block inside the mechanism were depressed according to the position of the holes in the card. The wires were attached to weighted strings which caused the correct group of warp threads forming the pattern to be selected.

New Jersey
Early nineteenth entury

**Woven Coverlet**
L. 86 in   219 cm
W. 72 in   183 cm
*Gift of Mr James Amster*

Jacquard coverlet woven of natural cotton and indigo and red wools. It is in two sections and joined down the middle. There is a fringe on two sides. The inscription in the lower left corner reading 'John B Welty, Boonsboro, Washington Co 1835' is that of the weaver.

Maryland

**Woven Coverlet**
L. 84 in 213 cm
W. 72 in 183 cm
*Gift of Mr and Mrs S. Collins*

Jacquard coverlet woven in natural cotton and red, indigo and blue/green wools. The two sections are joined and there is a fringe on three sides. The inscription reading 'Jacob Armbruster, Miami Co, Ohio 1839' is that of the weaver.

The pattern of lilies and starbursts is very similar to that used for other coverlets woven in Ohio about the same time.

**Woven Coverlet**
L. 80 in   203 cm
W. 77 in   196 cm

This Jacquard coverlet has been woven in two sections and joined down the middle. The warp is of natural cotton and a vibrant red wool whilst the weft is of indigo and medium blue wools. It is fringed on three sides. The border showing a series of houses was one often seen on Ohio coverlets. It is interesting to see the tulip in the two lower corners with the inscription 'H. Petry Canton' around it. Petry was a professional weaver of Scottish descent.

Canton, Ohio
*c.* 1840

**Woven Coverlet**
L. 85 in   216 cm
W. 76 in   192 cm
*Gift of Mrs Mary M. Burnett*

Jacquard coverlet woven in two widths from natural cotton and indigo dyed wool. The inscription reading 'Benjamin Lichty Bristol Ohio 1848' is that of the weaver. It is fringed on two sides.

The original owner was a Mr Warner from whom the donor's father Joseph Richardson Miller received it. Mr Miller was born in Durham and emigrated to Pennsylvania with his parents.

**Woven Coverlet**
L.  101 in   257 cm
W.  88 in   224 cm
*Gift of Mrs Dorothy Olcott
Elsmith*

**Woven Coverlet**
L.  101 in   257 cm
W.  88 in   224 cm
*Gift of Mrs Dorothy Olcott*
*Elsmith*

One of the earliest dated coverlets in the Museum's collection, was woven by Harry Tyler, born of British parentage in Connecticut, who later in life lived in Jefferson County, New York. His trademark, a lion, was in use until 1845, when he changed it to an eagle. Tyler drew all his own patterns and worked alone, assisted only by his children. The dying of the yarns was done in a small building at the rear of the house and he used indigo for blue and cochineal for red. Monkeys and little dogs frolic beneath the trees in the border and in this instance the inscription 'L A Wright' signifies the person for whom Tyler wove the coverlet.

In addition to coverlets Harry Tyler wove ingrain carpets.

The coverlet belonged to Harriet Burton Ainsworth, great-grandmother of the donor, who married in 1834, John Nash Esselstyn in Cape Vincent, New York State, and it has been handed down from mother to daughter ever since.

New York
1836

**Woven Coverlet**
L. 88 in    224 cm
W. 79 in    201 cm
*Gift of Mr Paul L. Joseph*

Double cloth coverlet of intricate pattern woven from natural cotton and red and blue wools. It is fringed on three sides. The inscription reads 'Beauty of the West 1851'.

**Woven Coverlet**
L. 94 in   239 cm
W. 81 in   206 cm
*Gift of Mrs L. Boyd Hatch*

The blue dyed cotton used in the weaving of this coverlet has faded to a soft blue/green. The weft is red wool. It is joined down the middle and the red fringes have been added. The inscription, repeated three times, reads 'M. Stauffer 1851'.

**Woven Coverlet**
Square: 82 in   208 cm

Double cloth coverlet which has been woven in two strips and joined down the centre. Possibly the coverlet was originally indigo and white and had been dyed in the piece.

It is said that this coverlet was part of the trousseau of Rebekah Sharpless, born at Middletown, Delaware Co., Pennsylvania, who died of smallpox in 1780. She was to have married in 1771 but was 'put off on account of the man's disposition of mind'. As the coverlet is most certainly of nineteenth-century origin the story must be legend.

**Snowflakes**
**Woven Coverlet**
L. 84 in   213 cm
W. 78 in   198 cm
*Gift of Mrs Josiah P. Marvel*

This double cloth coverlet with a centre seam is made entirely of wool. Both warp and weft are of tan, indigo and lighter blue wools. The bottom is fringed.

The border is known as 'Pine Tree', a motif which was also used in crewel embroidery and on quilts. There are many versions of both the snowflakes and the pine tree patterns and during the nineteenth century they are often to be seen on the same coverlet.

Pennsylvania
*c.* 1840

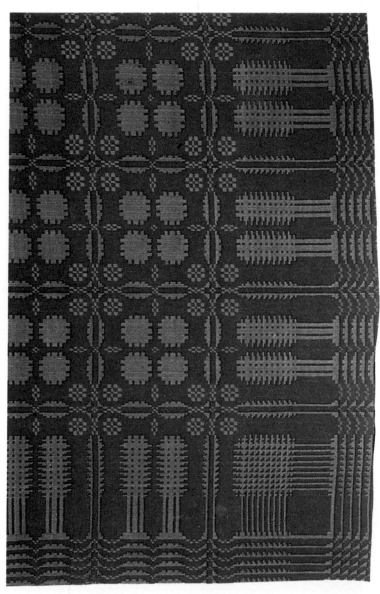

# Stencilled and Embroidered Bedcovers

Stencilled bedcovers were found mainly in New England and New York during the period 1820 to 1850 and were a development from the theorem paintings on velvet, a craft which was taught in many seminaries for young ladies. Such spreads were never made commercially and very seldom were they backed and quilted.

The first patterns were made up of many units which could be arranged to give a variety of designs. Later stencils were simplified so that a flower, for instance, would be painted from a single unit. These later stencils do not show the variations of the earlier ones. To give more detail some parts of the pattern were touched up freehand after the stencil had been removed.

The paint, which could be concentrated vegetable dye mixed with gum arabic, or a pigment bought from a hardware store, was tamped through the stencils, one colour at a time with a brush or with a pad of cloth.

Most embroidery of the eighteenth century was worked in the fine two-ply worsted or 'crewel' yarns which ultimately gave their name to a particular type of wool embroidery. In addition to bedhangings and coverlets, crewel yarns were used to embroider a host of smaller items such as chair seats, petticoats, aprons, pole screens and pocket books.

A view of the Stencilled Bedchamber showing a stencilled wall,
*c.* 1830, from the Joshua Lasalle House in Wyndham, Connecticut.

**Coverlet**
L. at longest point 94 in   239 cm
W. 102 in   259 cm

The stencilled bedspread has a central motif of a basket of red roses
with green foliage and there are smaller similar motifs in the four
corners. The two lower corners have been cut away to
accommodate the bed posts.

L. 101 in  257 cm
W.  90 in  229 cm

This quilt could have been made from the best pieces saved from a set of worn-out bedhangings. Many pieces of homespun linen have been joined together to make the top, which is embroidered with typical crewel work patterns of birds, fruits and flowers in shades of yellow, brown, blue and pink.

Part of the backing is a sepia-coloured block print fabric 'Farmyard', c. 1770, from the English Bromley Hall factory.

An approximate date of 1770/85 has been given to this quilt, although the embroidery could be earlier.

**Embroidered Top**
Square: 93 in    236 cm

A complete contrast to eighteenth-century embroidery, tops such as this were very popular towards the end of the nineteenth century. Here, six-inch squares of unbleached calico have been embroidered in outline stitch with quaint scenes of everyday life and homely objects. The pattern of the embroidery in the border is more sophisticated.

Late nineteenth century

## STUFFED WORK or TRAPUNTO COVERLETS

*It was not until the first half of the nineteenth century that 'all-white' coverlets became popular in the United States of America. They were made for decorative purposes rather than warmth and were very suited to the Greek Revival and Empire styles of furnishings. The making of an all-white quilt or coverlet where the attractiveness depended solely on the design, and stitchery, presented a far greater challenge to the needlewoman than the making of a patchwork one. Although the technique of stuffed work was introduced into the American colonies during the eighteenth century, it was not greatly used until the era of the all-white coverlet.*

*Fine cotton or linen in a plain weave was used for the top. The backing was of a coarser material and there was seldom an interlining. The background quilting was very fine with tiny stitches close together to give a stippled effect.*

*As with candlewick coverlets, designs tended to be similar.*

**The Colonel's Lady Coverlet**
L. 106 in 269 cm
W. 89 in 226 cm
*Gift of Mrs Thomas Riggs Cox*

The design of this all-white coverlet is rather different from most. A detail of the central medallion shows Liberty with flag, Liberty cap, drum, cannon and cannon balls; spread eagle in flight holding an olive branch and seventeen stars. A wreath enclosing the initials 'M.W.T.' and the date 1821 is at the top of the coverlet.

The maker was Mrs Alexander (Mary Waldron Nexen) Thompson, wife of Colonel Alexander Thompson, U.S.A., whom she accompanied to frontier forts in Indian Territory. They were hosts to General Lafayette at Fort Niagra in 1824. After Colonel Thompson's death his widow lobbied a bill through Congress to provide pensions for the widows of Army Officers.

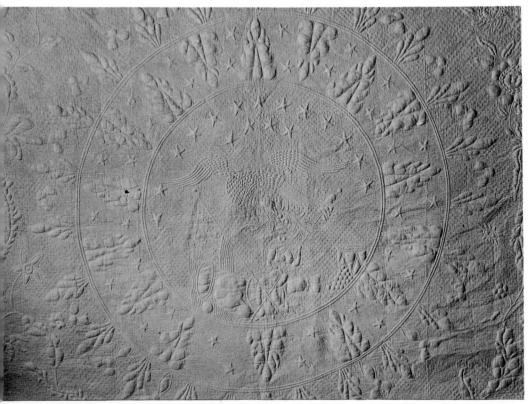

# Bibliography

Burnham, Harold and Dorothy. *Keep Me Warm one Night – Woven Coverlets in Eastern Canada*. University of Toronto Press and the Royal Ontario Museum, 1972

Carlisle, Lilian Baker. *Pieced Work and Applique Quilts at the Shelburne Museum*. Vermont, 1957

Colby, Averil. *Patchwork*. Batsford, 1958

Colby, Averil. *Quilting*. Batsford, 1972

Davison, Mildred and Christa Mayer-Thurman. *Coverlets*. Art Institute of Chicago, 1973

Finley, Ruth. *Old Patchwork Quilts*. Bell

FitzRandolph, Mavis. *Traditional Quilting*. Batsford, 1953

FitzRandolph, M. and F. M. Fletcher. *Quilting*. Dryad Press, Leicester

Graves, Sylvia. *History of Needlework Tools and Accessories*. David & Charles, 1973

Gutcheon, Beth. *The Perfect Patchwork Primer*. Penguin

Hake, Elizabeth. *English Quilting*. Batsford, 1937

Hall, Eliza Calvert. *A Book of Handwoven Coverlets*. Little Brown & Co., 1914

Harbeson, Georgiana B. *American Needlework*. Bonanza Books, New York, 1958

Holstein, Jonathan. *The Pieced Quilt – An American Design Tradition*. New York Graphic Society Ltd, Greenwich, Conn., 1975

Ickis, Marguerite. *The Standard Book of Quiltmaking*. Dover

Jones, Stella M. *Hawaiian Quilts*. Honolulu, 1973

Montgomery, Florence M. *Printed Textiles, English and American Cottons and Linens 1700–1850*. The Viking Press, New York, 1970

Orlofsky, Myron and Patsy. *Quilts in America*. McGraw-Hill, 1975

Petrie, Sir Flinders. *Decorative Patterns of the Ancient World*. Quaritch, 1930

Safford, Carlton and Robert Bishop. *America's Quilts and Coverlets*. Dutton & Co., New York, 1972

Waring, Janet. *Early American Stencils*. Dover, 1968

Betterton, Shiela. *The American Quilt Tradition*. Catalogue of Bicentennial Quilt Exhibition. The American Museum in Britain

Betterton, Shiela. *American Textiles and Needlework*. The American Museum in Britain, 1977

# Index

THE AMERICAN MUSEUM IN BRITAIN, the only comprehensive museum of Americana in Europe, is located at Claverton Manor, a country house near the city of Bath. The house, situated above the valley of the river Avon, was designed in 1820 by Sir Jeffrey Wyatville, architect to King George IV.

The museum tells the story of American life from about 1680 until 1860 through a series of completely furnished rooms, some of which have original panelling brought from the United States. Contrasts in the life of colonial New England are shown in the Puritan Keeping Room of the 1680's and the cosy tavern kitchen of the 1770's with its beehive oven and well-protected bar, in the blue-green panelled living room from Lee, New Hampshire, and the mid-eighteenth-century parlour of Captain Perley, who led his Minute Men at the battle of Bunker Hill. The sophistication of the parlours from Colchester, Connecticut and Baltimore, Maryland, introduces the period of the New Republic. An early nineteenth-century country style bedroom contrasts with the elegance of the Greek Revival dining room of New York and the richly ornate bedroom from New Orleans at the time of the Civil War.

In addition there are galleries devoted to the American Indian, the Pennsylvania Dutch, the religious community of the Shakers, and the isolated Spanish colonists of New Mexico. There are further exhibits on the Opening of the West, Whaling (with a Captain's cabin reproduced from the last of the great Yankee whalers), Textiles (with a fine collection of quilts and hooked rugs), Pewter, Glass and Silver.

The Park and formal gardens provide an ideal setting for outdoor exhibits including a Conestoga wagon and an Indian Tepee. The old stables, adapted to make a gallery, house the Folk Art collection; nearby is a replica of George Washington's rose and flower garden at Mount Vernon, Virginia, and on the terrace is a herb garden and herb shop.

Further information may be obtained from The Secretary, The American Museum in Britain, Claverton Manor, Bath, BA2 7BD. Telephone Bath (0225) 60503.